DICK KING-SMITH'S
ANIMAL FRIENDS

For Myrle
D. K~S.

For Deirdre and Lucy
A. J.

First published 1996 by Walker Books Ltd
87 Vauxhall Walk, London SE11 5HJ

10 9 8 7 6 5 4 3 2 1

Text © 1996 Foxbusters Ltd
Illustrations © 1996 Anita Jeram

The text has been typeset in Cochin.
The titles have been typeset in Bernhard Modern.

Printed in Hong Kong

British Library Cataloguing in Publication Data
A catalogue record for this book is available
from the British Library.

ISBN 0-7445-3771-1

DICK KING-SMITH'S
ANIMAL FRIENDS

Thirty-one
True Life Stories

ILLUSTRATED BY

ANITA JERAM

WALKER BOOKS
AND SUBSIDIARIES
LONDON • BOSTON • SYDNEY

me, not so long ago,
at a friend's farm

Foreword

me, aged 2½, on our front lawn

I THOUGHT I WOULD TELL YOU ABOUT SOME OF MY ANIMAL FRIENDS.

Ever since I was very little, I've enjoyed the company of animals, big and small. I can still remember the thrill of riding on an elephant at the zoo when I was four, and the excitement of getting my first white mice.

As a schoolboy, I was mad on pets, and even as a wartime soldier I kept chameleons in North Africa and a puppy in Italy.

In my new school uniform, aged 9

After the war came twenty years of farming. I was married by then, with three children, and we lived in the country surrounded by all sorts of beasts and birds.

Later, as a presenter on children's TV, I worked with loads of different creatures, from chickens to chimps, from pigs to pythons.

It's not surprising that I like to write stories about animals. This is a book of little tales about a few of my animal friends.

Aged 36, with Monty, my pig

Some I was very fond of and knew for the whole of their lives, like Dodo the dachshund or Frank the rabbit.

Some I only had for a very short time, like the golden pheasants.

And some, like the two badgers or Midnight the angry cow, weren't all that friendly to me!

But all were interesting – one way or another – and each was unforgettable. I've enjoyed writing about them.

If you enjoy reading about them,

then everyone's happy!

List *of* Stories

The Elephant Ride

I REMEMBER, WHEN I WAS QUITE SMALL, GOING for a ride on an elephant at the zoo. I imagined we were in the jungle, and a tiger would appear.

I would be quite safe, of course, on top of the elephant. All the same I think I was quite glad to see my mother appear instead and wave at me.

No Luck

WHEN I WAS ABOUT EIGHT, I HAD a tortoise. I didn't know if it was male or female. By day it plodded slowly about on a patch of grass. At night I put an upturned wooden box over it: to keep it warm and dry, to stop it wandering off and getting lost, and to protect it from eagles. (There weren't any eagles where I lived, but I had seen a picture in a story-book of an eagle carrying off a tortoise.)

One morning I discovered that my tortoise was a she. I lifted up the wooden box and there beside her was a little round egg, like a miniature table tennis ball.

I didn't say anything to anyone about the tortoise egg, but took it into our house and upstairs to the airing-cupboard (the hot cupboard, we called it), where sheets and pillowcases and blankets were all laid out, on slatted wooden shelves in the warm darkness. I put my egg carefully between some nice thick blankets.

I wasn't sure how long it took for tortoise eggs to hatch out, so I kept on going to look at it, every day for ages and ages.

I didn't realize you had to have a father tortoise as well as a mother.

Tree Frog

ONCE, LONG AGO, I WAS given a green tree frog. All I can recall about it is that it was very small, bright green in colour, and had suckers on the ends of its fingers and toes so that it could climb up a pane of glass.

Catching the Skipper

ONE OF MY GRANDFATHERS WAS a very keen lepidopterist; that's to say someone who collects butterflies and moths. I don't think this happens so much nowadays. I hope not.

He had a beautifully made mahogany cabinet with dozens of slender drawers in it, each containing trays on which the bodies of hundreds of different butter-flies and moths were carefully mounted, their wings spread, their colours as in life.

SKIPPERS Hesperiidae ♂♂♂

He was a very kind and gentle man, my grandfather was. Yet somehow he never appeared worried at the thought of killing all those lovely insects. He caught each one in his butterfly net and then put it in what we called a "stink-bottle", a jar filled with some poisonous stuff which gassed it.

One day he took me with him to try to catch a small brown butterfly called a Lulworth Skipper, so named

because it had first been discovered at Lulworth Cove in Dorset. At that time my grandfather had a car called a Clyno, a dignified sort of machine that didn't go very fast, especially when he was driving.

At twenty miles an hour it took an awfully long time to cover the hundred-odd miles to Lulworth, and when we arrived at last and began to comb the steep sides of the cove, there was no sign of a Lulworth Skipper.

After a couple of hours, just as we were about to give up and start the long, slow journey home, up fluttered a little dingy brown butterfly.

Quickly my grandfather handed me the net (I was a good fifty years younger, so a lot faster than him). Off I dashed, and swung the net,

and caught the Lulworth Skipper.

We came,

we saw,

we conquered!

A Palace Fit for Mice

I USED TO KEEP MASSES OF PET MICE.
Many of them I bought from a mouse
farm in South Wales, where you could buy more than
forty different colours of mice.

I became a member of the National Mouse Club
(subscription 7s. 6d. a year – that's about 37p) and I
wore a little badge with a picture of a
mouse under the letters N.M.C.

But what I liked best about keeping mice was building cages for them. The cages I built were nothing less than mouse-palaces. They were very big, with glass fronts so that I could see my mice running about, and inside there were two floors with stairs connecting them, and lots of little walkways and bridges so that the mice got plenty of exercise; and, of course, there were cosy sleeping-boxes in the upstairs part – bedrooms where mother mice could have their children (and a great many children they had).

Some people find it restful to watch fish in a fish tank. What I liked best was watching mice in a mouse-palace.

A Short Stay

WHEN I WAS ABOUT FIFTEEN OR SO, I WAS LUCKY enough to have a wonderful place to keep some of my pets. It was an unused grass tennis-court, that had been fenced around with chicken-wire, sides and top, to make a huge cage. In it I kept lots of guinea-pigs and rabbits, and a tortoise or two.

One unforgettable day I was given two new pets: a pair of golden pheasants. Like many hen birds (who need to be camouflaged while they're sitting on their eggs), the female golden pheasant is quite a drab colour, a yellowish brown barred with black.

But the male golden pheasant is a magnificent-looking fellow, with a very long tail and brilliant feathering of gold and scarlet. On his head is a glowing yellow crest and, on his shoulders, a fiery amber cape or ruff above dark green patches. You can't imagine a more colourful bird. This one minced around his mate with little high-stepping strides, his ruff raised, and gave a shrill whistle.

You can imagine my feelings of delight when these pheasants – my pheasants – arrived that morning.

23

But you certainly can't imagine what I felt like later in the day. In the roof of the wire run there was, unknown to anyone, a hole where the wire had rusted away. The golden pheasants found it.

That evening I went to feed them, and they were no longer there. The rabbits and the guinea-pigs hopped and scurried about as usual, and the tortoises slow-marched around, but the pheasants were gone.

The hen bird had disappeared altogether, but the cock was sitting in the top of a tall tree nearby, his colours brilliant in the light of the setting sun. There was nothing I could do, no possible way of catching him.

I could only stand and stare. By the morning he'd gone. I never saw him again.

More and More Rats

Nobody much likes rats. They are thought of as vicious, cunning, smelly carriers of disease. Pet rats, on the other hand, are very clean and easy to handle, and make fascinating companions.

I know that the pair I once had couldn't have been more likeable. They were Japanese Hooded Rats, pure white on the sides and legs, but with a black head and a black line down the back.

I called them Jupiter and Juno, after a Roman god and goddess. Jupiter was quite a bit bigger than Juno. He was very tame and liked to travel around, sitting on my shoulder.

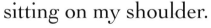

26

Juno was usually too busy for that sort of thing.

Busy?

Doing what?

Having babies.

In her first litter she had ten cubs. In her second, twelve. In her third, sixteen.

What happened to all those young rats, I can't remember – it was so long ago.

But I do remember old Jupiter very clearly, perched on my shoulder, tickling my neck with his whiskers.

He specially loved digestive biscuits.

Cabbage

Once, in Durban, in South Africa, I was standing on the upper deck of a ship, watching the cooks chucking out waste food from the galley below into the sea. As I watched, the most enormous shark (I don't know what sort it was) swam up, opened its huge mouth and took in a cabbage. Then it spat it out again.

I don't think it was a vegetarian.

28

Chameleon-hunting

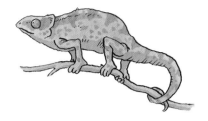

BEING BITTEN BY A CHAMELEON IS A FUNNY feeling. It doesn't really hurt at all. It's more of a grip than a bite. It's as though someone is pinching your finger with a pair of pliers, but very gently.

Before a chameleon bites you, it threatens you with a gaping mouth, sometimes hissing and swaying angrily from side to side.

Once I had a big cardboard box full of chameleons, about twelve of them. I'd better explain, in case you think that's a cruel way to keep them.

It was during the Second World War, and we were driving west along the top of Africa, from Cairo all the way to Tripoli. Every evening, when we stopped, I went chameleon-hunting, and I soon filled my box.

I only kept them in it while we were actually travelling. When we stopped, I took them all out and put them on a bush or a low tree branch, so that they could catch flies and other insects, which is what they eat. Just in case they didn't have any luck, I swatted lots of flies and put them in the box.

There was no danger of losing my chameleons.

They moved so slowly that it was
a job to catch them at it.

But there's one bit of a chameleon that
moves like greased lightning. A chameleon's tongue
is as long as its whole body, not counting the tail.

Here's what happens. Chameleons live in trees.
They creep along a branch (terribly slowly), holding on
to it with their prehensile tails, and with hands and feet
that are split so as to grip tightly.

Along comes a fly and settles, so it thinks, well out
of chameleon range.

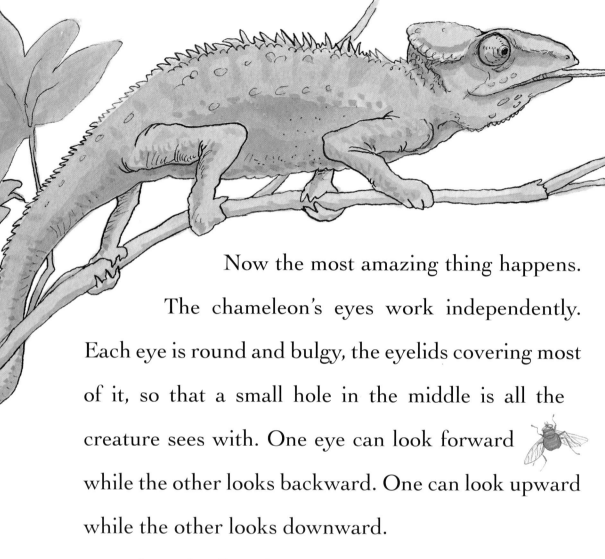

Now the most amazing thing happens. The chameleon's eyes work independently. Each eye is round and bulgy, the eyelids covering most of it, so that a small hole in the middle is all the creature sees with. One eye can look forward while the other looks backward. One can look upward while the other looks downward.

Back to the fly. There it is, cleaning its legs perhaps, while the chameleon focuses on it first with its right eye, then with its left. Then, like a bolt from the blue, out shoots the whole length of that clubbed sticky tongue, and it's goodbye fly.

Everyone knows the other thing
about the lizards called chameleons.
They can change their colours.

My chameleons stayed mostly brownish if they were in the cardboard box or sitting on the knees of my battle-dress trousers. On bushes they went greenish, on sand, yellowish.

At night they were usually cream-coloured with yellow patches. And when excited, they turned a sort of reddish-brown with golden spots. When they were really angry, those golden spots turned black.

33

I was fascinated by them, and didn't mind
how often they bit me. As time went by, they
became used to me and treated me more kindly.
Just before we got to Tripoli, I let them all
go. I didn't think they'd enjoy coming
on the invasion of Italy.

I sat watching them move away,
very very slowly, into the bushes,
hands gripping, feet gripping,
tails gripping, eyes swivelling.
Somewhere inside each mouth
a catapult tongue waited,
coiled like a spring.

I watched till every last
chameleon was gone
from sight.

Killed on Active Service

I HAVE HAD A GREAT NUMBER OF DOGS, many of whom lived to a good age. But one died young, killed on active service.

It was 1943, and we were fighting our way up the mountainous west coast of Italy.

Somewhere, in a hilltop village, I came across this puppy, for that's all she was, and bought her with a couple of packets of cigarettes.

She was a very Italian-looking puppy, smooth and slender and the colour of milky coffee; a kind of terrier, but more whippety. I called her Vicky.

She travelled with us for some weeks, ate well, and was much spoiled by everyone. Then I had an attack of jaundice and had to go back to Naples, to hospital.

When I got back to the battalion, they told me Vicky had been killed. She'd run across a road straight in front of a lorry. I never saw her grave because we'd moved on, but apparently they'd given her a proper burial and a wooden cross on which was written:

Vicky, Grenadier Guards

Lazy Ben

I ONCE OWNED A BULL NAMED BEN. HE WAS AN Aberdeen Angus, which meant that like all his breed he was deep-bodied, short-legged and hornless, with a shiny, satiny, coal-black coat.

Ben was also very lazy. Now you shouldn't ever trust a bull – of any breed – but I don't think Ben would have hurt a fly. It would have been too much effort.

When Ben was in the cowshed, he wore a stout leather strap around his neck, like a giant dog-collar, with a length of chain fixed to it.

But one fine summer's morning, when the cows had gone out to grass and Ben was left alone in his stall, he managed to slip his head out of the collar. Whose fault it was I don't remember, but either I or my cowman, Francis, hadn't done it up tightly enough.

The cowshed had three doors and all of them were wide open, but Ben couldn't be bothered to walk as far as the nearest one.

He simply put his great head against the wooden outer wall of the old cowshed, and pushed.

I know, because I was sweeping the yard and saw it.

In circuses they used to have dogs that were trained to jump through paper hoops. That's what it looked like as, with a loud splintering noise, first Ben's head and then his body, came clean through the wall, with pieces of wood flying everywhere.

Very slowly, so as not to waste energy, Ben ambled

into the nearest field and began to graze.

Before I could do anything, I heard a wild

shout of anger, and Francis, arriving back

from breakfast on his old bicycle, pedalled

past me and out into the field.

Throwing down the bike, he

ran after Ben, who, alarmed by

the angry shouts, began to trot

away and even at last to break

into a lumbering canter.

Right across the skyline they ran as I watched; but the

bull was fat and slow, and the cowman was lean and fast.

He soon caught up with Ben.

The last I saw before they
disappeared behind a hedge
was Francis grabbing hold of the end of Ben's tail and
pulling back on it like a man in a tug-of-war team.

I took the bull-pole and ran to meet them, but it wasn't

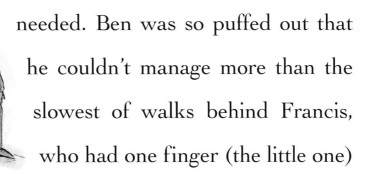 needed. Ben was so puffed out that
he couldn't manage more than the
slowest of walks behind Francis,
who had one finger (the little one)
crooked through the ring in the bull's nose.

We tied him up again, making sure the collar was tight
enough, and set about mending the cowshed wall.

As for Ben, he gave a great sigh and
flopped down, worn out.

Susie

Susie was a small, hairy, black-and-white terrier. I got her from an old chap called Jack when she was about the size of a guinea-pig.

Later, she grew bigger than that, but not much.

Susie was always very short-tempered, growling at anyone who said things like, "Get off my chair, Susie."

She loved me best but she growled at me just as much. She followed me everywhere.

If I was ploughing, Susie would trot behind the plough in the newly-turned furrow, up and down the field, all day long.

42

During her long life she had numerous brushes with death, but there's one I remember above all the others.

One Boxing Day – a bitterly cold day it was, with a biting east wind – Susie went missing. The days passed with no sign of her, and sadly my wife and I resigned ourselves to the fact that at last her luck had run out.

Eight whole days later, as I came out of the back door of the farmhouse to go and start the morning milking, I saw a filthy, bedraggled little object dragging herself painfully up the yard.

We could only suppose she'd been stuck somewhere deep below ground, and perhaps had to wait till she became thin enough to struggle free.

43

To have survived eight days and nights in freezing weather with nothing to eat was just believable, but with nothing to drink? Impossible – for any dog except Susie.

We cleaned her up and fed her on warm milk, glucose and egg, and within a day she was her old self.

We couldn't have been more pleased to have her back, but if Susie was pleased too, she never showed it. She just growled at us, and snarled at all the other dogs as usual.

Badger-
biffing

I BET THERE AREN'T MANY
people who can say, "Once I biffed a
badger on the bottom with my hat."

I can. I was going out early one summer's
morning to fetch the cows in for milking.
On my way I had to cross a big pasture,
and there, right in the middle of it,
was a badger.

Now badgers are nocturnal animals and, though there was a big sett in the nearby wood where we often heard them clucking and chattering at night, it wasn't often that we saw them in broad daylight.

So I hurried towards this solitary badger, hoping that it wouldn't run away till I'd had a good look at it. It didn't run away. It didn't take the slightest notice of me, even though I was now standing right beside it. It just carried on snuffling about in the grass.

I felt rather foolish. I took off my hat and biffed the badger gently on its bottom.

It didn't even look up. "What's up with you, my friend?" I said. "You deaf, or blind, or both?"

Slowly, with that rolling bear-like shuffle that badgers have, it began to move towards the wood, while I continued to beat a light tattoo on its backside. Until, at last, it came to a hole in the hedge, and disappeared.

The very next morning I went exactly the same way to fetch the dairy herd, and there, in exactly the same place, were two badgers. My friend, I thought, and his friend!

Happily I ran towards them. With a volley of furious grunts, the two badgers charged at me. I fled at top speed.

Nobody ever believes this story.

But it's true.

47

Dulcie Maude

Jinks

Lupin

Three Special Cats

DULCIE MAUDE

OUR FIRST SPECIAL CAT WAS A TORTOISESHELL-and-white queen called Dulcie Maude, who had, in her lifetime, one hundred and four kittens.

What's more, she liked to have them in unusual places such as a hay-filled manger in the stables or, on one occasion, in a large cardboard box half-full of electric light bulbs.

The most comfortable place that Dulcie Maude ever chose was in a loft where lots of unwanted old things were stored. One of these was a doll's pram that still had its little pillow, blue blankets and pink eiderdown in it.

The doll had long disappeared, but in its place Dulcie Maude lay purring happily in the pram, nursing yet another brood of children.

HIGH JINKS

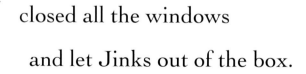

THE SECOND SPECIAL CAT
I remember was a ginger female by the
name of Jinks. Jinks lived to be very old – I can't
remember how many kittens she had.
But I do remember first bringing
her home as a kitten herself. She'd
been born in a warehouse and she was
really quite wild so, before I took her out of the box
I'd carried her home in, I made sure that the room
we were in was escape-proof. I shut the door,
closed all the windows
and let Jinks out of the box.

It was lucky it was summer and there was no fire in the grate, because the kitten dashed straight up the chimney.

What wasn't so lucky was that the chimney needed sweeping, and down came an avalanche of soot. By the time I'd managed to reach up inside the chimney and grab hold of the kitten, I was covered in the stuff.

As for Jinks, she had changed colour completely, from ginger to coal-black.

LOVING LUPIN

THE THIRD OF MY SPECIAL CATS WAS ANOTHER
ginger – long-haired this time and a tom. His name was
Lupin and in fact he belonged to one of our daughters.
But when she and her family went to live in America for
a year, Lupin came to stay with us.

Lupin was special because he was in some ways more
dog than cat. He bossed our dogs about, and when we
took them for walks, Lupin would come too, marching
along behind, waving his plumy tail.

And there was another way in which he was different.

Most cats like to keep themselves to themselves, accepting admiration and affection from their owners but not giving much back. Lupin was very loving. He would rub his big round furry face on ours, purring like a steam-engine and making quite a fuss of us. But we were only the cat-sitters. When his real owner came back after that year in America, you should have seen the fuss that Lupin made of her.

Talk about true love!

Nanny Anna

People think that a dachshund is just a sort of short-legged, long-bodied dog. They do not realize that there are dogs … and there are dachshunds.

Dogs like to please their owners by doing what they are told. Dachshunds like to please themselves.

Our first ever dachshund was called Anna, and when we got her as a puppy, she took not the slightest notice of anything we said to her.

"She must be stone deaf," we said.

But she wasn't. She was just a dachshund.

Apart from being as stubborn as all her breed, Anna's speciality was mother-love. Quite early in her life she began to be called Nanny.

It wasn't just her own puppies that she fussed over.

She did not need to be in milk, she just came into it at the drop of a baby. Kittens were well received if there was a cat crisis. And once she tried to play mother to four piglets.

A young sow had rejected them, but Nanny thought that they were lovely and immediately settled down to nurse them in her basket. Alas, newborn piglets, unlike puppies, have sharp little teeth, but still Anna put up with them till they could be fostered on to another sow. She saved their lives, in fact.

The Pig Harness

THE FIRST PIG I EVER OWNED WAS A PEDIGREE Large White called Molly. Molly was not only beautiful and intelligent (as all pigs are), but very sensible and easy-going.

At that time I only had one old pigsty, and I didn't like to see her confined in it – I wanted her to have more freedom. Equally, I didn't want to spend a lot of money on pig-fencing. Looking in a farming magazine, I hit on the solution: a "pig harness".

I sent off for it.

The harness consisted of stout leather straps that buckled round the pig's body, and were then attached to a length of chain that looked strong enough to anchor the *QE2*.

The chain ended in a huge expanding spring, and the spring was fixed to a great steel spike that was driven deep into the ground with a sledge-hammer.

Once harnessed, the pig could then move freely in a large circle around the spike, so far but no further. With help, I fixed the straps around Molly's large white body. She stood patiently for the fitting, her attention held by a trough full of food.

Then the harness was
attached to the chain which
was attached to the spike.

Her food finished, Molly moved slowly off in her
new outfit, until at last she reached the full limit of the
chain and came to a full stop. She grunted, and
strained against this mysterious thing that was
holding her back.

"No use trying to

bust that, old girl," I said.

"That spike and that spring and

that chain would hold an elephant."

Molly's reply was a loud squeal of anger.

Then she pitted all her strength

against the pig harness.

The spike held firm.

The spring,

now fully expanded,

held. The chain held.

But suddenly all the stout leather

straps and buckles burst apart,

and Molly trotted

happily away!

Midnight

I ONCE BOUGHT A BLACK COW, THE BLACKEST COW you ever saw, coal-black, raven-black, black as midnight (which is what I called her).

Sharp and curved were Midnight's horns, and seeing her in the sale ring I was reminded of pictures of the fighting bulls of Spain.

For some strange reason she went very cheap, and I was pleased with my bargain when the haulier delivered her in time for the afternoon milking.

What a milking that was.

At the first touch of the first cup on the first teat, Midnight exploded into a burst of kicking that stripped the milking machine into its component parts and left me battered, bruised and breathless.

The sheer ferocity of the animal was frightening: she leaped and pranced and bawled in anger. Her fierce eyes blazed and there was no doubt about what she would have done with those twin daggers on her head if the neckchain hadn't restrained her.

A few days later she charged my wife, who had to get under a fence in a great hurry.

"What happened?" I said.

"She put her head down and started to paw at the ground, and then she gave a horrible kind of roar and came straight for me."

"She'll have to go," I said.

She went.

Tortoise-riding

LOTS OF PEOPLE, INCLUDING ME, CAN SAY THEY'VE fallen off a horse at some time. But how many can say (as I can), "I've fallen off a tortoise"?

It was, of course, a giant tortoise.

Most giant tortoises live in the Galápagos Islands, in the Pacific. Actually, the tortoise I was riding was not from the Galápagos, but from an island in the Indian Ocean called Aldabra.

I'm not sure which tortoise is the bigger – the Aldabra

or the Galápagos – but this one was certainly big enough.

I sat astride its huge, shiny shell, and said, "Gee-up!"

Nothing happened.

Then, with a sudden lurch,

the tortoise took a large step forward.

I fell off backwards and landed

on my bottom with a bump.

Alas, Poor Evil

My brother once had a ferret called Evil. Evil was a hob (a male ferret), his long snaky body the usual dirty yellow colour, his eyes pink. Despite his name, he was quite good-natured with people he knew.

But one fine day Evil somehow escaped from his hutch and went missing. A search was mounted, but there was no sign of the ferret.

Later, a friend of my brother's called Jeff was rummaging about in a shed, looking for something or other, when, under a pile of old rubbish, he came upon Evil, and grabbed hold of him.

Evil was not best pleased.

He bit deep into the ball of Jeff's thumb.

That evening (the ferret now safely back in his hutch) Jeff went to his doctor for an injection. His mind was full of thoughts of blood-poisoning or even rabies, leading to a painful death.

In fact he suffered no ill effects.

But that night Evil died.

Goats on the Bed

I USED TO KNOW SOME PEOPLE WHO KEPT A lot of goats. They lived in a bungalow (the people, I mean, not the goats).

One day, on my way to visit them in their garden, I walked past their bedroom window and happened to look in. There, lying happily on the bed, chewing the cud, were two large nanny-goats.

I mentioned this to the people.

"Oh, no!" they said. "Crumbs in the bed are bad enough, but goats' droppings are the limit!"

68

Tree Fox

NOT FAR FROM THE COTTAGE
where we live now is a long, narrow spinney,
threaded by a small stream.

My wife and I were walking along the edge of it one
late September morning when we saw a fox – a dog fox
by the size of him – slip into the far end of the spinney.

When we entered by the same gap, we were
surprised to see no sign of him; and though
our three dachshunds – Dodo, Poppy
and Little Elsie – marked his line eagerly,
they lost scent and interest
a little way in.

70

This scene was replayed on several walks,

and always the dogs lost the scent at the

same place, beneath a big old crack-willow.

As such trees often do, it leaned out over the stream,

its thick trunk at an angle of forty-five

degrees to the ground.

We never found an earth in the spinney, so always

presumed that the dog fox, on hearing or scenting us,

simply slid out on the far side and away.

Till one day, standing beneath the willow,

we chanced to look upwards.

There he sat in a comfortable crotch

fifteen feet up, paws together, brush

curled neatly round him, ears pricked,

looking down on us.

What a patronising look it was.

We left, feeling small.

Walking Frank

I'VE OWNED DOZENS AND DOZENS OF rabbits, of many different breeds, but Frank is the one I'll always remember best. He was a French Lop, a very big kind of rabbit with drooping ears. In colour he was what's known as a Butterfly Smut – whitish, with lots of brown spots and patches, and on the muzzle a butterfly-shaped marking.

At the time I also had a number of Dutch does, quite small black-and-white rabbits, and Frank became the father of the oddest collection of children.

Some were black-and-white, some brown-and-white, some had smuts on their noses, some didn't. Some had sticking-up ears, some had hanging-down ears, and some had one ear up and one ear down.

Frank loved his food. I weighed him once when he was in his prime and he tipped the scales at eight kilos. He was so big that I knocked three hutches together so that he didn't feel cramped.

I used to exercise him too, on a collar and lead. Frank liked these walks. Often he'd suddenly do a great buck-jump in the air to show his pleasure. The problem was that, though taking a dog for a walk means that the dog goes where you want, taking a rabbit for a walk means going wherever the rabbit chooses.

And Frank always chose the vegetable garden.

Leslie

DRIVING HOME ONE NIGHT, WE SAW, IN THE HEAD-lights of the car, a hedgehog in the middle of the road. The lights and the sound of the approaching car had caused it to roll up into a ball.

Hedgehogs have it firmly in their minds that if they're rolled up, they're safe. They may be safe from some predators, but not from cars or lorries.

I picked up this hedgehog in a bit of old rag, and we took him home. Or we took her home; we couldn't tell. So we called him, or her, Leslie, a name that serves for a boy or a girl.

Leslie spent that night in a spare rabbit-hutch, and by the next morning was quite ready to have a good drink and a meal of tinned dog-meat, which hedgehogs like very much.

For several days we kept him or her, hoping that if he or she got used to us, he or she might stay when we released him or her into our garden. Hedgehogs are very useful in gardens because they eat slugs and snails.

One evening we gave Leslie a last good meal, then put him or her down on the lawn, and watched as he or she trotted away. Ours is a walled garden. What we didn't know then was that hedgehogs are good at climbing walls.

We never saw Leslie again.

Bribery

I WAS ONCE ALLOWED TO HOLD A BABY FEMALE chimpanzee in a safari park. I sat on a bench, and she sat on my knee, put her arms around my neck and gave me some rubbery kisses.

We were getting on really well together until the little chimp spotted Dodo, my miniature red wire-haired dachshund, who was underneath the bench. The chimp reached down a long arm, and I could see her thinking – I'm going to pull that dog's hair.

Dodo flinched away, and I could see her thinking – that creature is going to pull my hair.

The chimp pulled Dodo's hair.

Luckily I had come prepared for naughty behaviour. I took a packet of Polo mints out of my pocket and the chimpanzee instantly forgot all about the dog. She took each mint from me delicately between thumb and forefinger, popped it into her mouth, crunched, swallowed, and held out her hand politely for more.

How I would have loved to take her home with me.

How unhappy Dodo would have been.

Eric

ONCE I CARRIED AN INDIAN PYTHON, draped round my neck, for about half an hour. His name was Eric.

Eric was not a really big python. At his thickest part he was about as thick as a man's thigh, and he was about ten feet in length. Some pythons can be more than twice as long as this.

People think that snakes are cold and slimy. Eric's skin was warm and dry, and it was easy to feel the power of the thousands of muscles in his beautifully marked body.

I wore him around my neck and shoulders like a giant scarf, and he was heavy, I can tell you. But he behaved perfectly, and I didn't feel the least bit nervous of him.

Except perhaps towards the end of our meeting, when Eric began to feel he'd had enough.

At least I think that's what he was trying to say when he started to squeeze my neck, just a little. I handed him back to his keeper.

The Hitch-hiker

WE WERE ONCE DRIVING TO WEST Wales, at the start of a family seaside holiday, when we saw something very small and yellow waddling along the middle of the road in front of us.

It was a duckling.

It was quite alone, and appeared determined to go to the seaside, too. So we gave it a lift and some chocolate cake. And afterwards we brought it home.

Solomon and Albert

I ONCE KNEW A LLAMA THAT HATED a zebra. Or was it a zebra that hated a llama? I'm not sure. All I know is that they were not the best of friends.

They lived in adjoining paddocks in a private collection of animals, separated by a high chain-link fence. On one side was Albert the llama, and on the other was Solomon the zebra. Every day they would put on the same performance, just like actors in a long-running play.

First, Albert would come up to the wire and stick his head over it, and he would stare at Solomon with that sneering, toothy, condescending stare that llamas have.

Solomon would notice, of course, though he pretended not to. All the time he'd be grazing his way gradually over towards Albert.

Eventually Solomon would come close enough for Albert to do what he'd been wanting to do.

Angry llamas have a nasty habit of spitting at those they do not like, and when Albert judged Solomon to be near enough, he would spit at him.

At precisely the same instant, Solomon, with a shrill neigh of fury, would whip round and lash out at Albert with his hind hooves, trying to catch him on the chin. I never saw either of them score – it was always a goalless draw. Solomon's heels never quite reached Albert, and Albert's spit never quite hit Solomon.

But each lived in hope that one day he'd succeed.

The Stowaway

On a cruise my wife and I took to the West Indies, there were about thirteen hundred people – passengers and crew – aboard the ship, and one pigeon.

It was a perfectly ordinary-looking pigeon, bluish-grey and pink-legged, just like any one of the thousands of birds you see in city streets and squares.

But this was a very clever pigeon.

In no time at all it found out that not only do people on cruise liners eat a lot – they also spill and drop a lot of food on deck.

The pigeon made itself at home on the lido deck, where many of the passengers came to sit outside for breakfast and lunch. Every day, throughout these mealtimes, it strutted about underneath the tables, pecking up bits of food that had been dropped, sometimes on purpose. Some thoughtful person always put down an ashtray filled with fresh water.

All the way across the Atlantic, the pigeon ate and ate, until it couldn't stand, but lay on its stomach.

Eventually, after weeks of feasting, it was put ashore.

But I wouldn't mind betting that it stowed away again on the very next cruise liner that called there.

Dodo: Star of the Show

OUR MINIATURE RED WIRE-HAIRED DACHSHUND, Dodo, was born on a farm in west Wales, and from the moment we picked her up to bring her home with us, it was plain that she was a most unusual dog.

Though so young and so small, she was very self-possessed. The first of our animals that she met was a Great Dane. He bent his huge head to this midget. She looked up and wagged at him.

Some years later, when Dodo was about five, something happened that changed her life.

A television producer was looking for a presenter for a small slot on a children's programme. She needed someone who had been a farmer and a teacher and wrote books for children (that turned out to be me), and who also owned a small, attractive dog (that was Dodo). Dodo and I must have made about fifty little films.

Though I improved as time went on, Dodo didn't need to: she was immediately at home in front of the cameras.

Not only did she like people, so that she always got on very well with the film crews, but she was always extremely likeable herself.

At first, the crew came often to our cottage, for we filmed a number of animals there or nearby, and they always arrived promptly at nine o'clock on a Thursday morning.

By a quarter to nine each Thursday (and only on Thursdays), Dodo would be waiting by the door for them to arrive and admire her.

Don't ask me how she knew. I don't know.

After a while Dodo began to be recognized in public. In London once, I suddenly heard some children crying, "Look! It's Dodo!" and they rushed up and made a fuss of her, which she loved; not because she was vain but because she was always so friendly to everyone.

And it wasn't only children who recognized her.

The guard of an Intercity train once came to punch my ticket (and hers).

"Why," he said, "if it isn't Dodo!"

She was always the star of the show.

Joe Crow

THE LATEST ANIMAL IN MY LIFE IS SITTING on the wall below my study window as I write. Now and again he looks up with a bright, considering eye. He is a young crow, not long fledged. We call him Joe.

I first met Joe a week ago. He was hopping down the lane. "Can't you fly?" I said, and for answer he did, not very well, but well enough to get on to my garden wall. A couple of hours later he was outside the back door, flapping his wings and opening his beak in a gesture that said plainly, "Feed me! Feed me!" Where his mother and father were, I don't know, but it was plain that I was expected to take their place.

Now Joe is always waiting for bits of soaked dog-meal.

I feed them to him beside the greenhouse.

After he's eaten, Joe goes up to the side of the greenhouse, sees another Joe reflected, and pecks angrily at it.

He's growing stronger and flying better by the day. Not surprising really, because our friends who live on the other side of the lane (a hundred yards as the crow flies) tell me that they are busy feeding a young crow who keeps asking for food. And our next-door neighbours say the same. No fool, Joe.

But we think of him as ours because he spends each evening with us. We sit out in the garden, talking, and Joe sits on the fence behind with his head on one side, listening. And at night he roosts on our roof.

Postscript

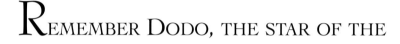

Remember Dodo, the star of the show? It might be nice, I'm thinking now, to end with a mention of another miniature red wire-haired dachshund called Little Elsie, who is sitting watching me.

Why? Because Little Elsie is Dodo's grand-daughter.

She's quite a different character from her granny – not as jolly and outgoing, less sure of herself (though she's as fierce as a lion when left in charge of the car); in fact not the film star type.

94

But the older Little Elsie grows – and she's really quite old now, though still very active – the more she gets to look like her grandmother. Her red coat has paled with age, her beard and moustache are fuller, her muzzle is grey.

And lately a funny thing has begun to happen. We keep calling Elsie by the wrong name. Several times a day, one or other of us will say, "Come along, Dodo," and along comes Little Elsie, wagging her tail and doing her special trick, which is to bare her teeth in a grin of pleasure.